The ANTI-RACISM Journal

Questions and Practices to Move Beyond Performative Allyship

Faitth Brooks

anti-racism educator and activist

PAGE STREET
PUBLISHING CO.

PAGE STREET
PUBLISHING CO.

FOR TO BE FREE
IS NOT MERELY
TO CAST OFF
ONE'S CHAINS,
BUT TO LIVE

CONTENTS

Introduction

I was the type of kid who never wanted to see anyone left out. I would go out of my way to play with the kid who was not as popular as or accepted by other kids. Inclusion has always been important to me. I had no idea my simple desire to include people and see people treated with fairness would lead me to a career of advocacy.

I come from a family of activists—my grandparents were actively involved in the Civil Rights Movement. It's only fitting that I would pick up the torch and become an activist too. The more I learned about racism and injustice, the more I was motivated to do my part and fight injustice. I realized I wanted to see everyone included; due to systemic racism (racism in schools, the workforce, housing, healthcare, and more), I saw the ways people of color were left out, and I wanted to be a part of the solution. I began writing about injustice and sharing my thoughts on Facebook, my WordPress blog, and Instagram. I wrote to anyone who would listen about the importance of fighting racism and injustice.

Over the years, my career as a director within nonprofits, philanthropy, and racial justice, as well as an audience of people who find what I have to say interesting and trustworthy, have catapulted me into my current career as an anti-racism educator and activist. After having many conversations with white folks about race and asking people questions about where their thoughts and ideas about race and racism originated, I realized many people held onto guilt and shame about their ignorance, or even their racist actions at times. I still believe there is hope for people to learn, grow, and change. I decided to create this journal for people to have a safe place to reflect and process.

While I am writing this from my perspective as a Black woman living in the United States, I think these questions also apply to other communities of color, specifically the Asian American and Pacific Islander (AAPI), Middle Eastern, Latine, and Indigenous communities. Our lived experiences differ, but all of our communities are impacted by colonization in some way. This is important to highlight as you work through the journal. With that said, it is imperative for me to mention that anti-blackness exists worldwide, even within other communities of color, and Black people still bear a great burden living in societies unwilling to honor their dignity and humanity.

Every day that Black people find themselves in spaces with predominantly white people, white people ask hard questions of Black people about race and racism. But these are questions they should be asking themselves, and this journal is your opportunity to do just that.

I created this journal to help you reflect on your views about race and racism and how you can contribute to creating a more just and equitable community. This journal is not all-encompassing of each ethnicity's intricate history. I encourage you to learn the history of Black, Indigenous, People of Color (BIPOC) communities as you grow in your allyship journey.

This journal is split into seven sections; each section has a challenge, reflection questions, and homework for you to continue your time of introspection. To build a strong foundation for your journey, the first three sections focus on internal reflection and understanding where your thoughts and ideas about race have been formed. The last four sections are meant to help you learn how to apply what you've learned to your daily life. The homework is meant to further your education and help you better understand the concepts presented, and I hope you will do the work to engage in it. Keep in mind, each challenge section is meant to be brief, which means you will need to do your part to learn more about the concepts shared at your leisure.

In 2020, in the heat of protests and injustice, people flooded the social media pages of activists with supportive messages, questions, and promises to help. Six months later, they were gone. I wondered: *Had they forgotten? Had they only wanted to appear supportive? Did the work get "too hard"?* This prompted me to ask the question, "Is your allyship conditional?" and I began a dialogue online via Instagram. Conditional allyship only speaks when it believes there is little to no social risk, while authentic allyship is willing to speak even when the cost is high; conditional allyship quickly returns to comfort when things get hard, while authentic allyship leans into the discomfort.

More than just me asking the question for an online audience, I think it's important to give those wanting to do something space to ask themselves tough questions like "Who taught me about race? Where did I learn stereotypes about other cultures? Why does racism still exist?" Let's be honest—most people who are learning what it means to acknowledge the racism that exists within them need a place to process. It can be embarrassing, disappointing, and frustrating to recognize the flawed ideas you once believed and the negative perceptions you had of people of color. This journey will require you to grow in self-awareness so that you can move from being self-focused to becoming an authentic ally.

Allyship requires action. Allies know that thoughts and prayers are not enough. "I'm sorry" is not enough. Re-posting a quote is not enough. Acknowledging a person's human rights and dignity and choosing to believe racism is a human rights issue is the most basic, foundational starting place for allies. Treating people with dignity and respect is not something you should expect pats on the back or awards for. You are merely doing what white people should have done a long time ago. We as humans should, at the minimum, respect one another. Here's the hard truth you must know: The work will continue with or without you. The white majority has yet to muster the courage to relinquish control and truly fight systemic racism. Many people would like to believe they are brave enough to do the right thing even when it's hard, but they are *not* brave enough. I hope you are one of the courageous ones.

When you have completed answering the questions in this journal and thoughtfully read and watched the homework, I hope you will be transformed into more than just an ally. I write this guided journal in hopes that you will become more of an accomplice or co-conspirator. You will no longer watch from the sidelines, saying "I got you" or "keep up the good work." You will be driven to do your part in actively dismantling systemic racism in your life and the local community. The actions we take locally spur into global impact.

Whether you see yourself as an ally or co-conspirator, remember that none of those words are feel-good terms that imply you've arrived. Your goal is not to be regarded as one of the "good white people." White people must be willing to walk in deep humility and remain teachable. None of us knows it all. Let go of the belief that you have it all figured out and understand someone else's lived experience;

unless you've lived it, you will never fully get it. If you begin to believe you have "arrived" as an ally, you have missed the point of fighting white supremacy. This way of thinking leads to acting out in entitlement, which displays a lack of humility. You cannot do anti-racism work and center yourself. White people, even if they have had proximity to Black people, do not know the extent of the racial discrimination Black folks face. Even though non-Black people will never fully understand our lived experience, they can empathize and choose to change their thoughts and behaviors. Everyone can still DO something.

It's now time to ask yourself some important questions that will indicate where you are on your anti-racism journey and where you want to go.

By embarking on this journey of self-reflection, I hope that you are taking your next step in divesting from a system of whiteness that you benefit from. I am happy you desire to challenge yourself to be better and do better. Here's the thing—you can't give up. Getting honest with yourself will be hard. Resist the impulse to throw your hands up and say, "Oh well, this is harder than I thought. I wanted to be an ally, but now my family won't talk to me, and my best friend is no longer in my life."

If you have engaged with my work in any capacity, you know that you must be ready to lose something. I don't wish family break-ups or strained relationships on anyone, but I want you to know up front that it's a possibility. Not everyone will get it, not everyone will listen, but it's still the right thing to do. There will never be a good excuse for racism. There will never be any form of reasoning to justify the oppression and abuse of another person. It's imperative for us to call out wrongdoing. Otherwise, people will become comfortable entertaining the dehumanization of other people, which we see happening every day on social media and in the real world.

Your opportunity to bail out on this journey is evidence of your privilege. Don't tap out and decide you don't want to speak up anymore, educate yourself, or change your day-to-day life. Don't get caught up in feeling overwhelmed and, as a result, do nothing. Look around you; you *can* do something. For instance, you can incite change in your own family/friend's circle, take on some of the education work that is foisted upon BIPOC by addressing those causing harm or overwhelming BIPOC, or create more equitable practices in the environments you frequent (like work or school). Building a better world starts with building a better you.

I believe in you and your ability to lay down your comfort to become a better co-conspirator. People want to know: *What should I do? What's next?* As you become reflective and self-aware, the customized answers to those questions will become clear.

Mindfulness and Activism

The more I engage in activism, the more I see how polarizing our world is because of our varying beliefs. There are chasms between us. Social media has only helped to reveal those divides and aid in our polarization. I am becoming more aware of the importance of mindfulness in our activism journey.

As a social worker, I discuss mindfulness often, and I've found mindfulness practices have helped me maintain longevity in activism. Mindfulness, used as a therapeutic technique, is a mental state achieved by focusing one's awareness on the present moment while calmly acknowledging and accepting one's feelings, thoughts, and bodily sensations.

Have you ever watched something or heard someone say something and had a physical reaction to what was said? Perhaps you felt tears welling up, you got angry, you felt frustrated, or you felt sad. I remember my friends talking about a case we saw on the news; their comments were so cavalier. Unfortunately, they had no idea I was a sexual assault survivor and that their words impacted me. To be honest, even I was surprised at how much their words affected me. I felt tears peeking through my eyes. I wanted to cry, but I did not want to cry in front of them. It was at that moment I realized I had some deep feelings to address. I wanted to be mad at them, but I knew my anger with them would be misplaced. Their comments were frank, but they weren't rude or downright disrespectful. They were supportive of survivors, but it was clear they had no idea what

I was going through. I decided to call my therapist, talk through what I was feeling, and explain how I was triggered to get to the root of the issue.

In the same way, I have witnessed white folks have visceral responses to conversations about race and racism. It is as if the discussion or even insinuation that they are racist is unbearable. I get it; who wants to be called racist? Yet, even well-meaning people are racists. Nonetheless, people respond in anger and fear. What triggered that defensiveness? Is there something that makes you ashamed to be associated with white people if you are white? Why is being called racist a trigger, especially if you did something racist? What made you feel you were immune or unable to display racist behavior?

We have watched white people melt down, like toddlers on a hot summer day, over BIPOC having a BBQ in the park, being in their own neighborhood, not speaking English, and a host of other incidents you can learn about through a simple Google search. All these incidents are external expressions of internal feelings rooted in fear and anger. Think of a time when you might have felt this way. In that moment, were you able to pinpoint what made you so angry? This is the practice of mindfulness. *How can I be present in my body and recognize my thoughts, feelings, and bodily sensations in this situation? What is triggering me? What is causing me to feel defensive?*

As you work through this journal, I want you to practice mindfulness because some sections are more challenging than others; some sections have more difficult questions to answer that will take you time to process. To get to the root of your feelings, perceptions, and behaviors, you must embrace mindfulness.

If you can, before you get started, take a moment to be silent. Find a meditation to listen to. Set your intentions, be open, let your walls down. Now is the time to invite introspection in. The beauty of this journal and process is that you are the captain of your own ship; no

one is reading this unless you open yourself up to group discussion. This is a personal journey. You get to cry, process, learn, and ask questions. This is the place to admit what you struggle to say out loud—or even feel ashamed of.

We have all made mistakes and changed our opinions and beliefs on things; this is not unnatural. If your thoughts and perceptions are changing, you are growing, and moving forward is better than standing still.

I want you to have a space to write your responses to the questions I asked you earlier so you can begin your mindfulness journey.

1. Have you been called racist? How did you respond? Were you defensive? What triggered that defensiveness? If you have not been called racist, how would being called racist make you feel?

Question

2. If you are white, have you ever felt ashamed to be associated with white people? If that's the case, why do you think so? Have you ever felt better about yourself because you were accepted by white people? Have you benefitted from proximity to white people?

Question

3. Why is being called racist a trigger for you, especially if you did something racist? What made you feel you were immune or unable to display racist behavior?

4. Have you ever paid attention to your body and noticed what triggers a physical response from you? When you are triggered, does it make you cry or want to cry? Does it make your stomach drop or your heart pound?

_____

_____

_____

_____

_____

_____

Question

5. Mindfulness can look like spending 5 to 10 minutes noticing feelings and sensations in your body, practicing silent reflection, or journaling. How can you incorporate mindfulness into your anti-racism practice? What would it look like to reflect rather than give a knee-jerk response?

Question

6. Write at least one thing you used to believe that you now feel embarrassed about and how that evolution in thought occurred.

"I conceived of the Center as an extension of Martin's personality, not just a place, not just a building, but a spirit, one undergirded with his philosophy of nonviolence and love in action. It would be the official living memorial, a place where we would teach his philosophy, methodology, and strategies of nonviolence in the hope of bringing about social change and eliminating what he called the triple evils of society: poverty, racism, and war."

—Coretta Scott King

7. How does shame or embarrassment feel in your body? How do you cope with your feelings and their physical manifestations?

HOMEWORK

For this section, I want to encourage you to purchase a book called *The Inner Work of Racial Justice: Healing Ourselves and Transforming Our Communities Through Mindfulness* by Rhonda V. Magee and read chapter 2, "Sitting with Compassionate Racial Awareness." This book highlights the importance of the inner work that helps us stay in hard conversations and work toward solutions. It is also full of tools to help guide you on your mindfulness journey, and it's perfect to read with a friend or book club.

What Did It for You?

When I first became a social work case manager, I was young, bright-eyed, and ignorant. It was my first time working in the foster care system. Over my years as a case manager, I sat through hundreds of court cases where the state determined what the course of a child's life would look like.

I used to think foster care was "cut and dry," and people lost their kids because they were abusive or irresponsible parents, but that wasn't always the case. It turns out that foster care has a vast gray area, and some incredible parents lost their children to the foster care system. Some biological BIPOC low-income families fought for the children to remain with them but lost them to white middle-class foster parents who would eventually adopt them. I observed the role classism played in determining where the child would stay long term.

Over time, I learned that I participated in a system that had many flaws and was determined to learn and grow by listening to the voices of those who mattered most—the children and the adult adoptees who began to speak out. The people directly impacted by my decisions and everyone else within the foster care system should be heard. It's my responsibility to listen and learn from them. I wouldn't have changed my opinion on the foster care system had I not watched what happened within the system while doing my job. In life, I believe we all have these "aha" moments that open our eyes to something we may not have seen, known, or recognized before. I think the same is true for many of you when it comes to racism.

Trayvon Martin. Eric Garner. Tamir Rice. George Floyd. Ahmaud Arbery. Breonna Taylor. Atatiana Jefferson. The Atlanta spa shootings. The El Paso Walmart shootings. Haitian immigrants at the border.

Which tragedy caused you to see that something is wrong? When did you finally see racism as a system where inequalities occur in legal, social, financial, and education systems? Why do you think it took you so long to open your eyes to the realities of BIPOC?

Were you taught to be color-blind? Why is that perspective problematic? How did the "color-blind" approach contribute to why it took you so long to see the issues at hand? Embracing the color-blind mentality means you don't really SEE me—a Black woman. To be color-blind is to ignore how I must move through this world as a Black woman in the United States. To be color-blind is to make the false assumption that this world treats us all the same. To be color-blind is to assume that if we all "work hard," we will be successful. Color-blindness ignores systemic oppression and hinders and stops the advancement of those in the Black community (and other communities of color). Color-blindness doesn't help you to be an ally. We need to talk about racism, and we need to talk about why our society devalues people of color. We need to talk about anti-blackness. But we can't do that if we're committed to being colorblind.

I need you to see me. I need you to see my pain. I need you to see the injustice and mistreatment that comes my way daily because of my skin color. I need you to see it so you will say something and use your power to disrupt white supremacy. Get uncomfortable and disrupt! Otherwise, we will raise another generation of children who refuse to "see" color and, in turn, repeat the same harmful cycles of racist behavior. We need to talk about our colors; they are beautiful. They represent many ethnicities and cultures. Acknowledging someone's color and heritage is a way to embrace their culture instead of erasing it. Denial erases, and seeing affirms.

In this section, you will reflect on the question, *"What did it for you?"* What was the moment that changed your perspective and caused you to wake up to the reality that something is not right and that you have been blinded to it?

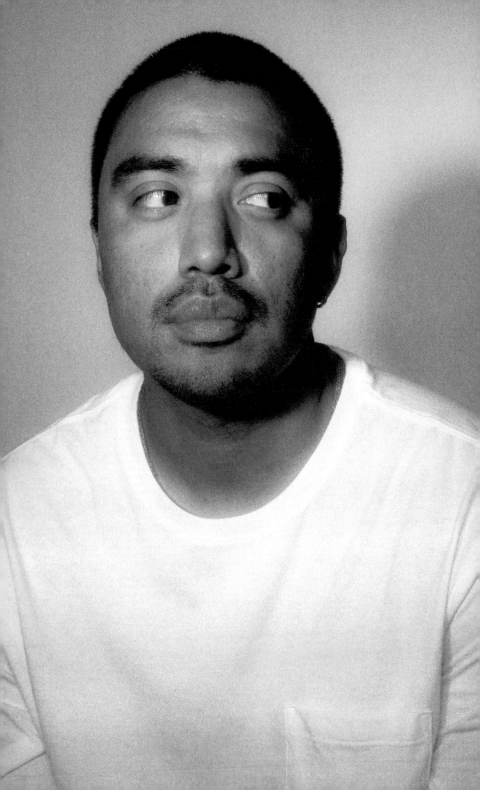

Question

1. Racism is real. When was the moment you "woke up" to acknowledge this fact? What movements or people helped guide you here?

Question

2. Conditional allyship only speaks when it believes there is little to no social risk, while authentic allyship is willing to speak even when the cost is high; conditional allyship quickly returns to comfort when things get hard, while authentic allyship leans into the discomfort. Up to this point, has your allyship been conditional? What conditions do you have? What consequences are you willing to incur?

Question

3. Who has been the most influential person in your anti-racism journey? What about that person's approach attracted you to them? How can you challenge yourself to listen to someone with a different approach? Have you talked to that person about their influence on your life and/or engaged with those sources?

What Did It for You?

Question

4. Do your social media posts about racism reflect tangible changes in your life? If not, how can you expand your work to produce more meaningful learning and engaged experiences?

5. Did you post a black square on social media or #stopaapihate, run for Ahmaud Arbery, or attend a BLM protest? If so, why?

Question

6. What are other tangible steps you can take to engage in anti-racism work? If you have the means to do so, have you donated to causes? Have you volunteered for organizations that support BIPOC? Are there other ways you're engaging in anti-racism work?

7. Did social media help you learn more about incidents of injustice and aid in your understanding of racism? If so, what did you learn?

8. In what ways has social media hindered your anti-racism journey? Do you ever feel like you will be canceled if you make a mistake? How are you working to address those fears?

HOMEWORK

As you conclude your reflection on what got you to this point, challenge yourself to think about how recent events caused many to rush to buy books on anti-racism. Ask yourself: *Did the act of purchasing a book make me feel like I was doing something? Did I read and consider the ideas in the book(s) I bought? Or did I just move on? How did the book(s) shift my thinking, if at all?*

READ THIS

"About That Wave of Anti-Racist Bestsellers Over the Summer..." by Katherine Morgan, Literary Hub, November 25, 2020
https://lithub.com/about-that-wave-of-anti-racist-bestsellers-over-the-summer/

"Did Last Summer's Black Lives Matter Protests Change Anything?" by Keeanga-Yamahtta Taylor, *The New Yorker*, August 6, 2021
https://www.newyorker.com/news/our-columnists/did-last-summers-protests-change-anything

Searching for Seneca Village

Since the early 1990s, historians and archaeologists have been working to uncover and reveal the story of Seneca Village. The historians Roy Rosenzweig and Elizabeth Blackmar were the first to study Seneca Village in detail and included it in their book *The Park and the People: A History of Central Park* (1992). Soon after, in 1997, the New-York Historical Society organized an exhibit curated by Grady Turner and Cynthia Copeland, *Before Central Park: The Life and Death of Seneca Village*, which further expanded on this history for the public.

These projects inspired a group of archaeologists and historians to wonder if evidence of Seneca Village still existed in Central Park. Led by Diana Wall and Nan Rothschild, they formed a group called the Seneca Village Project, now called the Institute for the Exploration of Seneca Village History (IESVH). After years of planning, research, and preliminary testing, they conducted an excavation in residential areas of the village in the summer of 2011 and uncovered significant remnants. In 2015, the Central Park Conservancy conducted additional research and archaeological testing while planning for reconstruction projects in the two playgrounds in the village area. This work added to the body of knowledge about Seneca Village, specifically its relationship to the history and landscape of Central Park. The IESVH also advocated for commemoration of Seneca Village and worked with the Parks Department, Conservancy, and Community Board 10 in Harlem to erect the nearby sign that has marked the site since 2001.

We know more about Seneca Village now than ever before, but there is more to learn. Research is ongoing to uncover the history of this exceptional community.

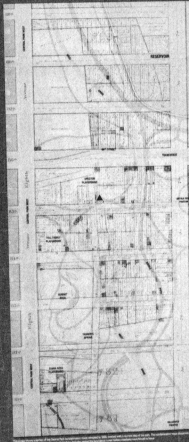

Historical Records

Our understanding of Seneca Village is based on various historical records. When the city began planning Central Park, it commissioned maps to document who owned and inhabited the land slated for the park, with details about the types of houses and other structures. Called the "condemnation maps," they were compiled in 1855 and used to determine who and how much to pay for each property. In the same year, New York State conducted a census, which can be compared with the maps to better understand who lived in the various houses in the village. The census includes information about race, profession, age, place of birth, and relationships among household members.

There is also evidence of Seneca Village in federal censuses, church records, tax records, municipal death records, newspaper articles, and documents related to the creation of Central Park. No photographs of the village have been found.

Archaeology

Archaeological investigations offer new insight into Seneca Village and provide a tangible connection to its residents. The excavations of 2011 involved eight weeks of work in the park, during which archaeologists and students collected several thousand artifacts and other cultural materials such as bone and shell. Many artifacts reflect the residents' domestic life, that Seneca Village was not a community of poor squatters, as it with often portrayed, but a relatively stable and bricks and stones were related to the construction of their homes. Analysis of these materials supports the understanding predominantly middle-class community.

Central Park is a protected historic landscape. It is listed in the National Register of Historic Places and designated as a New York Scenic Landmark. All work in the area is planned with consideration of the site's exceptional history and its potential for additional archaeological remains.

Redware artifacts discovered in 2011 included transfer plate, redware pipe bowl, glass medicine or perfume bottle, and one here from a domestic/local meal possibly a chop or quail.

Students excavating at the excavation in Seneca Village in 2011.

The Name "Seneca Village"

The exact origin of the name "Seneca Village" is unknown. It was recorded by Thomas McClure Peters, an assistant priest and later rector of St. Michael's Episcopal Church, who started a mission to serve the poor in the community; he later established All Angels' Church. In a book documenting the history of the church, Peters uses the name "Seneca Village" to describe a miserable settlement of low whites and colored people." In the "wastelands" that became Central Park, a depiction that perhaps served to justify the church's missionary work. Considering this derogatory characterization, one theory is that the name refers to the Native American Seneca people and was intended as a slur.

If the name "Seneca Village" originated in the African-American community, it could have been chosen for uplifting associations. One theory is that it was intended to evoke New York and the abolitionist movement there. Another is that the settlement was named after the Roman philosopher Lucius Annaeus Seneca because some African-American activists were known to have been inspired by his anti-slavery book, *Morals*.

Several 19th-century sources refer to the community as a part of Yorkville, the village that developed in the early 19th century further east and expanded in the 1830s following the construction of the New York and Harlem Railroad. The reservoir adjacent to Seneca Village was identified as located in Yorkville.

The Central Park Conservancy developed this program of reinterpretive signage based on research conducted by the Institute for the Exploration of Seneca Village History (IESVH), with additional research and content contributions by the Conservancy and funded Research, Inc. Project supervision by Marie Warsh, with graphic design by Douglas Riccardi. Sign fabrication by Pannier Graphics.

Rethinking the Past

I had a lovely childhood and upbringing, but there were rocky areas of my life. The truth is, there are some things we'd rather forget, and I had plenty I wanted to forget. When I finally decided to get therapy at 25 years old, I was nervous, but I was ready.

I knew the only way I could heal and move forward was to acknowledge the wounds of the past. My hurt and pain from years past would resurface if I did not face it head-on. It was easy to avoid the past, but I had to deal with the pain of the past living within me.

Once I was able to identify the pain of my past—my mistakes, my wrong thinking, my behavior—I could adjust, change, and heal. The longer I remained in denial and chose avoidance, the longer I denied the truth. The truth was that I was wounded. Once I realized I would always be bound to my pain if I never dealt with it, I decided to see it, face it, and name it.

We cannot heal from something we have not named.

We can all relate to that feeling, but sometimes certain things need to be called to our attention so we can remember. Not everything is better left unsaid, and not everything should be forgotten.

Some things should be remembered.

History keeps receipts. We can't isolate what happened in the past from our present. Sometimes we must go back and learn what we never knew to make sense of the present.

Why do we remember the Holocaust? Why do we remember the Genocide in Rwanda? We remember because history mustn't repeat itself. If we are ignorant of our history, we will forget and repeat history all over again.

In the United States, there has been no urgency from our government, churches, communities, or schools to remember the past and our racist history. Why aren't we fervently sharing the history of Japanese internment camps? The Native American genocide? Enslavement of Africans? Native American residential schools? In the United States, there has been a concerted effort to forget and conceal. There is a reason people used Critical Race Theory (a body of legal scholarship taught at the university academic level) as an excuse to ban accurate history and truth-telling in schools. What do those in power have to lose when people are informed?

Power and control.

Therefore, they have nurtured the creation of a blind apathetic society that repeats the same atrocities in new ways. There is no effort to help the next generation DO BETTER and BE BETTER. The selfish ambition of wealthy men with no vested interest in humanity has created a monstrous society of people willing to ignore the history of pain communities have endured for social status and "feel good" living that is void of accountability and truth-telling.

History matters.

The truth matters.

Now it is time for you to think about how your past has shaped you. What did you learn then, and what are you unlearning now?

Question

1. Think back on your youth. What was your impression of people from other countries? What did you think about Black people? Latinos? Indigenous people? Asian people?

Question

2. Think about your family members. What stereotypes did your family assign to communities of color (Black, Indigenous, Asian, Latine)? What did you believe those communities valued or didn't value?

3. Think about your neighborhood, the schools you attended, the community organizations you were a part of, the churches you attended, the teachers you had, the ethnicity of the dentists and doctors you visited, etc. Were you always part of the majority? Did you always or almost always see yourself reflected? If so, what advantages did that give you? What message did that send about who is worthy or unworthy?

4. What did you miss out on by growing up in a nondiverse community? If you grew up in a diverse community, what do you feel you learned?

Question

5. Are you more bothered by racist actions or racist attitudes? What forms of racism have you tolerated in the past?

Question

6. What aspects of your life have changed since embarking on this anti-racism journey? What aspects do you still hope to change?

Question

7. When you think about Black bodies, what feelings arise? Do you detect any fear? If so, where did that fear come from and was it taught to you? By whom?

8. As you reflect on your education growing up, did you learn about the real history of Black and Indigenous people in the United States? Did you learn the history of Latine and Asian people in the United States? Were you taught about the process of immigration and how it has evolved over the years and the ways the system is racially biased? If not, what are you doing to educate yourself now?

Question

9. Have you read about any controversies involving who decides school curriculums and how events in history are framed? Who should decide what history is and what will be taught?

HOMEWORK

Now that you have spent some time reflecting on the past, it's essential to see real-life cases where injustice has occurred in the present. You must begin connecting the dots to see how systemic racism is at work every single day. On Netflix, watch *When They See Us* and the follow-up interview with Oprah and the Exonerated Five. The Exonerated Five are one example of how racism has ripped apart real lives. Sadly, there are many other examples as well. We can't work to change things we are not aware of. Do some research to find other stories of late pardons or stories of people who sold cannabis and were convicted during the war on drugs, and are still imprisoned even as the newly legal industry of cannabis sales flourish.

Here and Now

Take a deep breath, close your eyes, and think about your life right here and right now. Let this sink in: You *will* be uncomfortable. You *will* make others uncomfortable. There will be a price to pay for speaking out.

I remember the moment I decided to talk about racism. I grew up in the South around conservative folks in the Bible Belt. Speaking out was an immediate death sentence to my social circles, and I knew it. I also knew my silence was only making the white people around me comfortable. If I wanted to address the issues, I needed to speak to them publicly. Yes, there was a loss, but I knew I would rebuild and make new friends. I can tell you with great confidence that standing up for the truth, speaking out, and confronting injustice was the best decision I ever made in my life and for myself. Not only did I find myself in a new way, but I also became a better person because I chose truth over comfort.

You may observe family and friends attempt to dismiss *Black Lives Matter*, immigration, the school-to-prison pipeline, climate change, protecting Native land, etc., and tell you that all of it is just a liberal agenda. Perhaps you've already spoken out and encountered opposition. You do not need to argue with people, but you need to remain engaged in anti-racism work within your community. Many of the laws and policies that will impact you directly happen on a local level.

Let's not forget racism is bipartisan.

Racism is not a Democrat or Republican, Liberal or Leftist thing.

Racism is a human rights issue.

If you find that people use their opinions or religious beliefs to discount a person's lived experience, you shouldn't listen to them. Racism is inexcusable. We should all aim to treat one another with dignity and respect, but there will always be people who find a reason to deny other people's humanity and will always have to fight this fight.

I've noticed that once the zeal wears off, people feel overwhelmed and burdened by the lack of "swift" change. "Did my protesting matter?" "Did I actually help change anything when I signed that petition?" When the fatigue sets in and you are ready to quit, you have to remind yourself of why you decided to care in the first place. No one enjoys tough times where things are mentally and emotionally difficult. It's tempting to back out when you are met with opposition from people who deny that racism is real. You may feel unqualified to address their ignorant statements or even correct them.

But ask yourself, are the people who are "opposing you" well read? Do they have facts to back up their argument? Do they have authentic, real-life relationships with multiple BIPOC, or are they finding videos online of a BIPOC or talking about their one "Black friend" to back up their racist views? Are they simply repeating what they've heard? When your thoughts and beliefs are challenged, use those moments to invite them into a space of dialogue or mindful reflection. Instead of trying to prove your point, ask them what brought them to their conclusions. What resources helped them to inform their beliefs? Finally, ask if they are open to hearing your perspective too. When two people are open to constructive dialogue rather than shouting matches, it's possible you may be able to hear one another's perspectives.

You will not change a person's mind with one conversation; think of your dialogues as an ongoing conversation rather than a fight to win. You can have differing perspectives and still treat people with

dignity. It's difficult at times, but my goal in anti-racism work is to treat people the way I want to be treated, which means I do not promote the use of dehumanizing and degrading language toward anyone. This doesn't mean I let go of healthy boundaries for myself when someone uses hateful or degrading language toward me, but it does mean I am mindful of the ways I use my words toward others. Words have power. Use that power wisely.

When you are armed with knowledge and education, you are more equipped to have difficult conversations. Don't back out now. Don't let fatigue persuade you to stay silent and step away from this. Racism thrives on ignorance and silence. Do not be part of that unhealthy cycle. I believe because you've decided to read this journal, you are ready to keep moving forward, even when it gets hard.

Question

1. List your losses. Have you lost anything since engaging in anti-racism work? Has it cost you anything? If you can't think of something, you are likely not yet swimming against the tide of racism.

Question

2. It has been said that if you have a brain, you have bias. We are conditioned to prejudge others based on our past experiences, media images, stereotypes, etc. What biases do you have toward Black people or other people of color? What assumptions do you make about BIPOC, and how do you fight against those assumptions?

Question

3. Have you ever noticed how many people of color are in your local community? Grocery stores? Library? Are you mostly surrounded by people who look like you? If so, when did you reach that realization?

Question

4. Is there a lack of diversity in your personal life? How do you explain it? How do you feel about it?

5. Why do you think Black women struggle with trusting white women? After you answer, read the article "Dear White Women" by Rachel Cargle (https://bit.ly/32O0XFO).

Question

6. What aspects of conversations about race feel challenging or daunting? In what ways do you see racist thoughts and actions still showing up in your life?

Question

7. What has the work of anti-racism challenged you to change in your life? For example, is your faith or academic community committed to anti-racist work?

Question

8. In what area of your life is it hardest to be an ally?
Why?

9. How have you dealt with racist comments from family members? What boundaries have you set?

10. How do you respond to people who don't understand #BlackLivesMatter, #StopAAPIHate, and other social movements led by BIPOC?

Question

11. When talking to other white people, what approach do you find to be the most effective in explaining the importance of anti-racism? It is likely that you will need to try different approaches to see where you can gain the most traction. The more you educate yourself and practice having transformative conversations, the more successful you will become in creating change. Think about common talking points from people who push back against anti-racism work. List them out and think about things you can share to counter those narratives.

12. The lynching of Black bodies should not be a spectacle. In our modern-day era, videos of Black people dying are often shown on social media to garner outrage and push for action. However, imagine the trauma Black people experience watching these videos. How have you been desensitized to Black death? Mass shootings? Hate crimes against the Asian community? How can you speak up for change without further traumatizing BIPOC in sharing these videos?

FREEDOM

OF OTHERS

NELSON MANDELA

HOMEWORK

While white folks can show enthusiasm for social justice work, it's also clear that some people are gatekeepers for patriarchy and power. In what ways have you been a gatekeeper? Are you willing to divest from your proximity to power? I'd love for you to listen to the podcast *Southlake*, where a school board and the town's parents are facing tension over the Cultural Competence Action Plan and a movement to end Critical Race Theory from being taught in schools. This podcast explores a broader topic of what happened in 2020 and where things are now on a local level. This podcast also explores how residents hopeful for a more diverse and equitable community continue to fight even when they are outnumbered.

LISTEN TO THIS

Southlake: https://www.nbcnews.com/southlake-podcast

Fears and Missteps

I hate making mistakes. It truly pains me to mess something up. I am also deeply empathic and become quite distraught when I realize my behavior has caused someone harm. My knee-jerk reaction is to lean into shame, which makes me want to run and hide. I immediately think: *What are people thinking of me? How do they perceive my actions? What do they think my actions say about my character and how I plan to fix my mistake?*

My mom taught me early in life to quickly ask for forgiveness when I make a mistake and never be afraid to address conflict head-on. While I have that sinking feeling in my stomach and my heart is pounding, I know the best path forward is to own my mistake.

I have a feeling you are stumbling through what it means to be an ally, paralyzed by fear of messing up, being called out and canceled on the internet, or being embarrassed for saying the wrong thing.

I hate to break it to you, but you are going to mess up.

You cannot avoid this.

It's not about IF you'll mess up—it's about WHEN.

No one likes making mistakes, yet we all make them. Sometimes you may not know what to say or do; you may find yourself tripping over your words, wondering if you are offending someone. You want to do better, but you are still unlearning harmful language, thoughts, biases, and behaviors. You are going to mess things up and say the wrong thing. You are still learning, and maybe you are beginning to see ingrained white supremacist thoughts and behaviors within you. When you've been raised to think a certain way, it takes time and intention to let go of harmful mindsets.

Did you know that there are plenty of people of all ethnicities influenced by white supremacy? There are people of color who uphold racist ideals about issues like colorism, xenophobia, and homophobia, which all have roots in white supremacy and create webs of oppression within each community. While they aren't the majority, some people of color must embark on the same journey to free their hearts and minds of harmful and dehumanizing thinking.

Go ahead and free yourself from any internal pressure you have been feeling. You are going to make mistakes in this work. Just because you will make mistakes does not mean that you should not be working hard to grow in your anti-racism journey.

We are all human and make mistakes.

What matters is that you walk in humility as you bounce back from your missteps. Remain teachable because you don't know it all. You have no idea what it is like to be Black in the United States, and you will never know. The experience of people of color in the United States is different from the white experience, and the trauma and history are different with each community. There is no way for me to replicate my experience for you to truly understand what it feels like. Everyone within my community has a different response to what we currently face. While it is okay to make mistakes, not everyone will react to those mistakes graciously. The people of color you know aren't just reacting to your mistakes, but to a lifetime of oppression.

James Baldwin stated, "To be a Negro in this country and to be relatively conscious is to be in a rage almost all the time." *Why is there rage?* I think we are tired of repeating ourselves and pleading with people to listen and care about our experiences and stories. We are tired of being gaslit. We are tired of seeing people make excuses for bigoted and racist behavior. We are tired of seeing the inequities of the justice system. We are tired of broken promises and abandoned diversity and equity action plans.

Enough is enough.

Don't use fear as an excuse to keep you from speaking up and being held accountable for your words and actions and choosing to do better. When you make a mistake publicly, you need to correct it publicly. It's not enough to slip into DMs and apologize privately.

If you hide behind your keyboard and get defensive, the act of humility and taking responsibility for your actions will not become second nature to you. You will skip mindfulness, you will skip assessing what is making you feel offended, and you will go on the defense. You will become convinced that whatever you do will never be enough. It is tempting to go down the rabbit hole of shame, but it's unproductive and you aren't helping to be a part of the solution. To be a part of the solution, you need to reflect and act. You need to be patient with yourself because you will not handle things perfectly all the time. But just like anyone else, you deserve grace to be extended to you as you learn.

We cannot shame people into caring.

Brené Brown, professor at the University of Houston and author, defines shame as "the intensely painful feeling or experience of believing that we are flawed and therefore unworthy of love and belonging—something we've experienced, done, or failed to do makes us unworthy of connection."

Shame and guilt will not cause people to care more.

Trust me, I have tried it; it doesn't work. Shame doesn't produce long-lasting results of change in a person's behavior, thinking, and actions. Some people display deplorable behavior and refuse to listen when called out. People are heavily influenced by their curated social media feeds, the news networks they watch, YouTube, and more. People consume content they like and not content they oppose or find questionable. Even though people often see things they agree with and rarely see what challenges their perspectives, there is still hope for people to change their mindsets; hope is not lost here.

Lead by example in the way you interact with people. Your behavior and actions will go a long way in influencing people to think and behave differently. So if you are thinking of addressing a friend or family member perpetuating racist behavior, remember that you can inform them, but if you shame them, it's unlikely they will change their behavior. You could say something like, "Hey, that statement is very offensive to the Black community. Please don't use that kind of language. I don't agree with those statements, and I will not be silent while you disrespect other people." You still speak up, act, and do your part. Eventually *some* people will follow and begin to do the same.

1. What are your fears about being a vocal and active anti-racist?

Question

2. How have you prioritized comfort in your anti-racism journey? How have you allowed fear to dictate what you say and do?

Question

3. How have you learned to admit and recognize when you are wrong? Have you been willing to correct your mistakes when called out?

4. What does it mean to you to commit your life to the work of anti-racism?

Question

5. Write about a time when you intended to be an ally, but you got pushback from BIPOC. What did you learn from that experience? Were you speaking over them? Were you misinformed or ignoring how they wanted to handle that situation?

6. Have you ever wished for praise, likes, or affirmation from BIPOC for your allyship or acknowledgment for your contributions?

Question

7. Name a time when you remained silent in the face of injustice. Why do you think you chose to stay silent? What has your silence cost others?

HOMEWORK

Now that we know it's not a matter of *if* you mess up but *when*, it's important for us to discuss how you can recover when you do mess up. Acknowledgment, an apology, and resisting defensiveness will help you bounce back after you make mistakes. Read this article and then reflect on a time you messed up. Think about how you responded. What would you change? What can you do differently?

READ THIS

"You've Been Called Out for a Microaggression. What do you do?" by Rebecca Knight, *Harvard Business Review*, July 24, 2020 https://hbr.org/2020/07/youve-been-called-out-for-a-microaggression-what-do-you-do

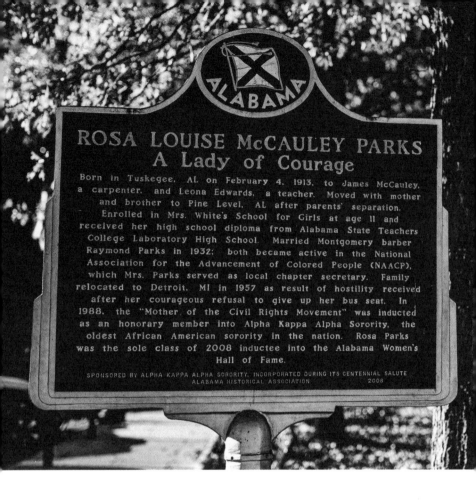

Finding Your Lane

I'm not going to lie, I think it's somewhat silly that teenagers have to decide what they want to do for the rest of their lives at age eighteen. We change and evolve so much; it's impossible to predict the type of person you'll be in 5 to 10 years.

It took a lot of trial and error for me to decide what I was interested in and passionate about. I knew that to discover my passions, I would probably have to try a few different jobs and internships. I think the same concept stands for activism. It's going to take a while for you to find your area of interest. Are you interested in voting rights, climate change, education, housing, immigration, equal pay/raising the minimum wage, or healthcare? Which areas are you drawn to learn more about? Which areas have local organizations you can volunteer to work with?

As you work on identifying your areas of interest, it's important to learn from BIPOC. There are a lot of Black folks in the activism space, leading organizations and sharing the ways people can support their work. Why are we always saying *listen and learn*? Because the voices of white folks have been centered for centuries. Pass the mic, please. We have solutions, community plans, and partnerships, and most of all, we have community support for our work. We have a lot to say, and our voices need to be amplified.

Train yourself to acknowledge Black people as credible sources on racism by simply believing them. For far too long, white people have looked to other white people to validate the experiences of BIPOC. We can speak for ourselves.

Performative allyship is easy to embody for the people overwhelmed by the work it takes to be anti-racist. Performative allyship seeks instant gratification from being seen as doing the right thing, looking for a pat on the back or a shout-out. Performative allies aren't deeply invested in the work; they are more likely to be defensive when "called in." When you are called in, people want to let you know what you did wrong and give you an opportunity to grow from it. Performative allies do not want to be considered racist but do not have the deep commitment to dismantle the system they benefit from. Are you willing to learn from BIPOC and not just take one person's experience as a representation for the whole community?

Posting to share and highlight injustice is excellent. We need that, but let me be clear, posting and talking about racism should come from a genuine and informed place. As we fight to combat misinformation, checking the source is important. Learning to find well-researched and trusted sources takes time; however, there are many respected academics who have been researching race and racism for decades. Find those voices. If you care about this work, you must do the work when no one is watching. Don't allow this to be a well-produced show for your social media audience or the people around you. Trust me, we know when it's not genuine.

If you want to find your lane in this work, you need to show you are trustworthy by being willing to learn and not seeking to be the center of attention. Learn how to accept your supporting role in this work. Can you leverage the support of your community to rally around the work of advocacy efforts BIPOC are leading financially? Can you donate your time, expertise, or money? Can you actively find ways to build financial and communal support systems for the work BIPOC are leading and need funding to continue? There are many ways to find your lane, and I believe answering the questions in this section will help you do just that. Remember that if you are not following the leadership of knowledgeable BIPOC, you probably need to keep searching for credible voices to connect with.

Question

1. Set a timer for one minute. List all the ways you have power and privilege. Then go back and brainstorm ways you could use this power and privilege to benefit BIPOC and change the status quo.

2. When you are anti-racist, you are willing to dismantle the system you benefit from rather than protect it. List three systems you benefit from (e.g., education, healthcare, housing). How have you been protecting this power structure? What steps can you take to dismantle this system? What work is being done by activists who are reimagining a different way of doing things?

Question

3. Who do you hope to influence the most in your work to be actively anti-racist? Where are you feeling frustrated in your current attempts to influence people?

Question

4. Is it easier for you to think you would be on the right side of history during the Civil Rights Movement in the '60s than to be on the right side of history in today's movement for Black lives? What are the obstacles people during the Civil Rights Movement faced, and how are they mirrored today? Are you afraid of getting arrested? Are you afraid of being tear gassed or beaten for attending a protest? Are you afraid of losing your job?

Question

5. What systems/organizations would you like to see dismantled? The prison-industrial complex? The military-industrial complex? The racist beauty industry, like skin bleaching? Do you want to defund the police?

Question

6. How are you staying away from performative allyship on social media? Do you find it hard to balance feeling performative and spreading awareness?

7. We have recognized the personal losses that will occur when you engage in this work. However, let's take a moment to acknowledge the gains. As you educate yourself and build authentic relationships with BIPOC, you will likely gain so much more than you lose. List what you will gain from doing this work. More importantly, consider some ways BIPOC would benefit from you divesting from white supremacy.

HOMEWORK

Now that the groundswell of energy to address the racism in our country is "settling down," people are finding reasons to disengage and check out. Hear me loud and clear: Now is not the time to check out and give up. If you want to find your lane, remember you must see and acknowledge the truth about racism. I want you to read this article about performative allyship and ways to move beyond it.

READ THIS

"Performative Allyship Is Deadly (Here's What to Do Instead)" by Holiday Phillips, *Forge*, May 9, 2020 https://forge.medium.com/performative-allyship-is-deadly-c900645d9f1f

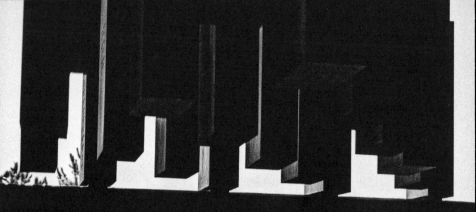

FOR THE HANGED AND BEATEN.
FOR THE SHOT, DROWNED, AND BURNED.
FOR THE TORTURED, TORMENTED, AND TERRORIZED.
FOR THOSE ABANDONED BY THE RULE OF LAW.

WE WILL REMEMBER.

WITH HOPE BECAUSE HOPELESSNESS IS THE ENEMY OF JUSTICE.
WITH COURAGE BECAUSE PEACE REQUIRES BRAVERY.
WITH PERSISTENCE BECAUSE JUSTICE IS A CONSTANT STRUGGLE.
WITH FAITH BECAUSE WE SHALL OVERCOME.

Challenge

Called In

In 2020, I felt a glimmer of hope I hadn't felt in a while. People were listening. It felt like, collectively, we may actually see change. The streets were filled with people of all ethnicities in support of Black lives. I felt like I was on a high after years of anti-racism work, years of being misunderstood, years of one-on-one conversations with well-meaning white folks. Years of being in a community with white folks and hoping some of them would trust my voice because of our decades-long friendship. I rarely talk about the ways I was impacted by the silence of white folks I'd spent years of my life being close to, only to see them post things in opposition to anti-racism. This made the already difficult work of activism feel even harder.

Nonetheless, I knew I needed to continue speaking out. This caused me to reflect on calling people *out* versus calling people *in*. Sian Ferguson states, "Much like *calling out*, calling in aims to get the person to *change their problematic behavior*. The primary difference between calling in and calling out is that calling in is done with a little more compassion and patience." I think there are times to call people out and then there are times to call people in. When you call people in, you give them the opportunity to learn and grow. In my mind, it's my way of holding out hope that people can be teachable and willing to change. Calling people in comes from a desire to see people do better. Instead of saying, "You messed up," you say, "I want to hold you accountable and help you grow so you don't repeat this behavior again." We are getting more polarized by the day, and I found that my anger and frustration increased as I saw people's promises go unfulfilled. The more we "moved on" as a country and opened back up, the less people focused on addressing racism. In fact, people made Critical Race Theory the new "Boogie man" and fought to change school curriculums.

Watching all of this unfold made the work feel impossible, and change felt like a distant dream. Hopelessness began to sweep in. I'd hoped people would fulfill their promises. I knew change would not happen as fast as I wanted it to, but I felt like people were forgetting. The global pandemic has impacted all of us in ways we will never forget. Somehow, I held out hope that people would finally put their blinders away and choose to see the evils of racism. I understand that people want to duck and run, not think about the bad in the world, and just focus on the good stuff. Life is sad and hard right now; people are tired and want relief. I get it, but I found myself thinking, *It must be nice for them to turn it all off; they can forget about this mess.*

People are fighting to forget, and we are fighting to survive.

You see, it's really tempting to avoid conversations about race. I get it—unpacking systemic racism isn't "fun," but we won't achieve equity for all without addressing the issues. As a Black woman, I can't escape the negative consequences I face because of my Blackness. Imagine what it feels like watching people use conspiracy theories and other reasons they find on news outlets or social media to excuse racism. And guess what? A lot of people buying into this harmful trap are people who were initially moved by the death of George Floyd and pledged to make a difference. They were performing allyship without being authentic allies. Genuine allyship takes work. Nothing worth fighting for is easy.

Holding on to hope can be difficult, especially when you see person after person murdered by police. You know that after years of outrage, barely anything has changed. Officers are still protected by the law, and that the prospect of people being held accountable seems grim. Promises of more cameras for officers, stricter policies, and fair trials fall on deaf ears. A lot of the time people wonder if an unarmed person did something that warranted them to be shot and killed. Is your advocacy and outrage against police brutality reserved for people who don't seem to be guilty?

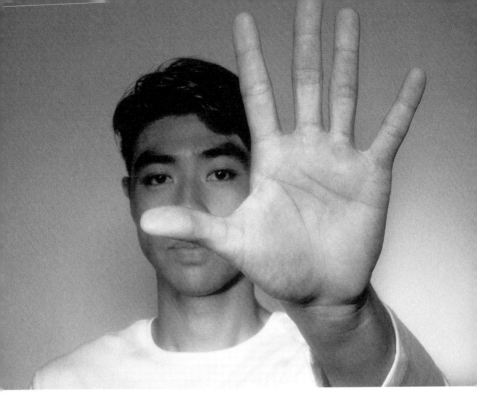

The work of anti-racism challenges us all; our thoughts, behaviors, and perspectives are all called into question as we examine our learned behavior. None of this is comfortable, but all of it is necessary. If we choose to, we can all be lifelong learners committed to fighting injustice. The more we are informed, the better we can advocate for ourselves and others.

When I find myself grasping for hope and dreaming of a better future, I am reminded that there are people willing to be called out and called in. When I think about the people who do care, I feel more hopeful, less angry, and more focused on the work at hand. While my anger is warranted in moments, I must remain hopeful. Keeping hope alive is what fuels my anti-racism work. If I have no hope that things can be better one day, then what am I fighting for? What are you fighting for?

Question

1. Why do you think it's important to learn
from BIPOC? Who have been your most
influential teachers? Who are you listening
to that challenges you?

Question

2. When someone implies that you have done something or said something racist, how do you react?

3. You cannot tell a Black person what it means to be Black in the United States. What are some ways in which you may be unconsciously gaslighting people? How do you respond when you see other white people gaslighting?

4. What is your default reaction when you become uncomfortable? How can you learn to push through?

Question

5. Do you believe people have to "deserve" justice before you feel comfortable speaking out against police brutality? Do you wait for "all the evidence to come out" before you denounce police brutality caught on camera? What criteria do Black people have to meet before you will advocate for their lives? Is your advocacy and outrage against police brutality reserved for people who don't seem to be guilty?

Question

6. In what ways is it tempting to oversimplify "Black perspectives" or "Latine points of view"? How do you challenge yourself to not take one BIPOC's perspective and assign it to the whole group?

Question

7. What facts and perspectives have challenged you
in this journey?

Question

8. What does it mean to decenter yourself as an ally in this work? List ways that you will do this as you work to become an ally.

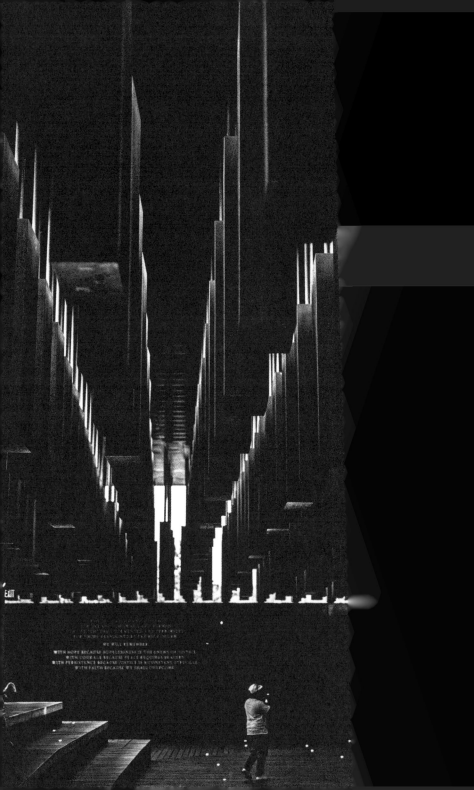

HOMEWORK

You've made it to the last section of homework. I want you to read this full article: *Calling In: A Quick Guide on When and How* by Sian Ferguson. As you read this article, reflect on what you are learning and on how you can implement the tools you're reading about in the article to your personal life. Remember that allyship is a journey; you will mess up, but it's important for you to recover and keep trying to improve.

READ THIS

"Calling In: A Quick Guide on When and How" by Sian Ferguson, *Everyday Feminism*, January 17, 2015 https://everydayfeminism.com/2015/01/guide-to-calling-in/

Conclusion: Where Do You Go from Here?

Congratulations! You made it to the end of this guided journal. I am so happy you committed to this process. Choosing to be anti-racist is a commitment to changing your life, attitudes, beliefs, and behaviors. It's choosing to acknowledge the tensions and pain many Black people and other people of color have experienced. It's choosing to open your eyes and see that George Floyd, Eric Garner, Tamir Rice, Atatiana Jefferson, Philando Castile, Breonna Taylor, and Ahmaud Arbery's deaths were not isolated incidents.

Self-evaluation is one of the most critical parts of your anti-racism journey. You cannot breeze past this. To be successful on this journey, you must commit to self-evaluation for the rest of your life. The racist ideas you've seen or been raised with are not going to disappear instantly because you "get it" now.

You will feel weary, and at times you will wonder if this is all worth it. It feels like everyone is fighting on social media: *listen to me, I am right, they are wrong*—you get the picture. It all gets overwhelming, and you are tired.

I know it's tough, but I want to encourage you to keep going. Don't keep going for me—keep going for YOU. Keep going because you believe your thoughts, actions, and behaviors matter. Keep going because you believe we need to dismantle systemic racism and you are tired of sitting idly by while people are lynched and killed in plain sight. Keep going because you want to chart a different path and leave a different legacy.

For many of you, you are not where you used to be. But remember there are people in your life who *are* where you used to be; therefore, you shouldn't look down on others who are "behind" you in this journey. The best thing you can do is focus on your journey of growth and change and be ready to point other white people in the right direction.

I do not know how to make all of this better, but I grow when I prioritize learning from others who are different from me. I grow when I learn Asian, Latine, and Native American stories. I challenge myself to grow when I can see the world from a different vantage point. I grow when I fight the urge to let fear guide me. I grow when I speak up and stand against injustice. I grow when I choose to hold out hope that things will not always be this way. I grow when I hold fast to the belief that we can build a better world one day. And even if no one sees the work I do, I still contribute to the change. There are millions of people who have committed to social change and equity. We don't know what everyone contributed, but their contributions matter and impact us today.

By the end of this, I told you that you would know *what's next* and that I wouldn't need to tell you the answers. This is not about me teaching you—it's about you committing to ask yourself the hard questions. I do still have one question for you, though. Is your allyship conditional? I hope by now you can confidently answer that question with honesty and humility.